This book belongs to:

_____

Copyright © 2018 by *Lauren Simone Publishing House*

All rights reserved. In accordance with the U.S. Copyright Act of 1976, the scanning, uploading, and electronic sharing of any part of this book without the permission of the publisher constitute unlawful piracy and theft of the author's intellectual property. If you would like to use material from the book (other than for review purposes), prior written permission must be obtained by contacting the publisher at laurensimonepubs@gmail.com.

Library of Congress Cataloging-in-Publication Data
Grant, Imani Ariana and Burchell-Kerr, Shaneika
Disco Balls of the Universe/ Imani Ariana Grant and Shaneika Burchell-Kerr
p. cm.
Illustration by Zachary-Michael Clarke and Simonne-Anais Clarke
Summary: Imani and friends attend a party in space and learn so much about the eight planets of the solar system.
ISBN-13: 9781948071161
ISBN-10: 1948071169
Title I.
2018930991

www.laurensimonepubs.com

Imani's Dedication

To my dad, Andre Kerr, who loves me unconditionally and believes in me

To my little brother, Nathaniel Kerr, who inspires me

To my supportive aunt, Karen Clayton

Way in the universe,
way up high...

There are eight planets in our *Solar System*. Each one shaped like a disco ball. They're all having fun dancing around the Sun. He is a star!

Back to *Earth*, my home,
for nutritious snacks and cool air.

Let's return to the party.

Why is it raining lava in here? Uh oh, it's *Mars*! Her face is so red, it looks like her volcano is about to explode!

Whew! Just in time, here comes *Jupiter*, the big, slow giant. He's so huge. No wonder his moves are so smooth.

Saturn takes over the dance floor, dancing to impress. Showing off her dusty, icy rings at best.

I have a strong feeling this party is about to end because I can't seem to see the *Sun* again.

Here comes *Neptune* dancing up a storm. Oh no, she is way too boisterous.

Let's go home.

Do you know why *Pluto* wasn't at the party?

Oh I know! He must be with the other *Dwarf Planets*.

The party has ended, but I had so much fun dancing with the planets.

What is your favorite planet?

KEY WORDS

Atmosphere: the air that plants, humans, and animals need to survive.

Boisterous: loud, noisy, energetic, or rowdy.

Dwarf Planet: a small object in outer space that resembles a planet.

Lava: hot melted rock erupted from a volcano.

Nutritious: food that is good for the body.

Planet: an object in space that rotates around a star such as the Sun.

Sun: the center of the solar system that causes Earth's light and weather.

Solar System: collection of eight planets and their moons in orbit around the Sun.

Universe: the solar system and space.

Volcano: a mountain or hill that has a crater for lava, rock fragments, hot vapor, and gas to escape.

FIND A WORD PUZZLE

```
V E N U S F O V K M E R C U R Y S
N T A D W A R F P L A N E T G S K
D R I N G S A B X H A K P A I X N
S W V V B E A R T H T K A O D F O
O V P L U T O G W A M I I N E B V
L P N E P T U N E Y O S A T U R N
A L T U F F F G Y V S H S S H X P
R A O S G J O P H I P L O N D U O
S N S T Z Q U G O X H S K Y W R W
Y E L A M S N J T V E L H U U A Z
S T B R R L I U J D R B Y X L N B
T S M S T G V P H S E A A I B U W
E X X S E D E I E P X L V O S S A
M L S U L X R T T A C M A R S F A
E A K N V O S E J C O X H J L P U
B V U U A Y E R J E E D K M J U V
U A O N A E O E R I V O L C A N O
```

Atmosphere	Mercury	Sky	Uranus
Dwarf planet	Neptune	Solar System	Venus
Earth	Planets	Space	Volcano
Jupiter	Pluto	Stars	
Lava	Rings	Sun	
Mars	Saturn	Universe	

DID YOU KNOW?

Mercury is the smallest planet but spins the fastest.

Venus is same size as **Earth**, but the hottest of all.

The **Earth** is the only planet with life.

It takes 365 days for **Earth** to orbit the Sun.

You can see **Venus** with the naked eye.

Pluto was once called a planet but now astronomers call it a Dwarf Planet.

Pluto has a heart shape on its surface.

YOUTH BIOGRAPHIES

Imani Ariana Grant
Imani is a 9 year old author who enjoys writing stories and playing the violin, basketball, and with her friends. She also enjoys figure skating, swimming, and dancing. Imani is also an entrepreneur, the owner of an online boutique store called Magitots. Follow Imani on Instagram @imaniarianag

Zachary-Michael Clarke and Simonne-Anais Clarke
Zachary is a 13 year old youth illustrator who loves animated movies, writing fiction stories, and creating graphic novels. He's excited to learn more about animation and cooking gluten free foods. He loves his pets and playing Animal Jam. Simonne is a curious16 year old youth illustrator who is passionate about the craft of story writing and sharing her stories with others. She loves animated movies and is studying how they are made. Follow on Facebook at https://www.facebook.com/SimonneAndZacharyArt/